TECHNO **TANTRUMS**

David Boyle is co-director of the New Weather Institute. He is also a parent of two children and became fascinated by the mismatch between the real and online worlds, after writing his book **Authenticity**. He lives in the South Downs.

Judith Hodge is a writer and editor with a particular interest in health and nutrition. She is also mother to a grown-up daughter, too old for Snapchat. She is planning a move to rural France but is worried about the wifi connection.

TECHNO **TANTRUMS**
10 STRATERGIES TO COPE WITH
YOUR CHILDREN'S TIME ONLINE

David Boyle
Judith Hodge

www.therealpress.co.uk

THE REAL PRESS
www.therealpress.co.uk
Published in 2017 by the Real Press.
© David Boyle and Judith Hodge

ISBN (print)   978-1912119677
ISBN (ebooks)   978-1912119660

"Some young adventurers from the mainland get lost or take a wrong turn and end up in here, trying to get to the island...

When they find the machines, with their perfect depictions of the adventures they should have been having, they become hypnotised. Some of them stand there until their lifeforce runs out, just hitting buttons, thinking they are rescuing a maiden from a dragon but really doing nothing at all.

You can't get their attention once they are hooked."

Scarlett Thomas, Dragon's Green

To Graham and family, for the original thought.

Contents

1 | INTRODUCTION
What would Steve say?

"We settle up and I go home to search for Kitty's
profile. I'm expecting tame stuff: updates to friends,
plus those blurry nudes. But, as it turns out, the
photos we talked about (artistic shots of Kitty in bed
or, in one picture, in a snowdrift, wearing stilettos)
are the least revelatory thing I find. In posts tracing
back to college, her story scrolls down my screen in
raw and affecting detail: the death of her parents,
her breakups, her insecurities, her ambitions. There
are photos, but they are candid and unstylized, like a
close-up of a tattoo of a butterfly, adjacent (explains
the caption) to a bruise she got by bumping into
the cash register. A recent entry encourages posters
to share stories of sexual assault anonymously."
About Kitty, 26-year-old bartender from New York City,
interviewed in New York Times about living your life
with total transparency.

Steve Jobs, the legendary CEO of Apple, steered his
company in the direction of making a great deal of
money out of British children. It may not have been
a conscious decision – in fact, it almost certainly
wasn't – but after Jobs died in 2011, Apple had
made so much money from UK schools spending the
Pupil Premium money on iPads, that it was used as
an explanation for Apple's profits at the company's

annual general meeting.

So it was strange to discover that Jobs' own children were banned from using iPads. This came to light when the New York Times technology writer Nick Bilton asked him whether his kids loved them. "They haven't used it," he said. "We limit how much technology our kids use at home."

Bilton gasped. This was heresy from the head of the IT Inquisition. "I had imagined the Jobs's household was like a nerd's paradise: that the walls were giant touch screens, the dining table was made from tiles of iPads and that iPods were handed out to guests like chocolates on a pillow."

He went on to interview a number of American tech leaders and found much the same. "My kids accuse me and my wife of being fascists and overly concerned about tech, and they say that none of their friends have the same rules," former Wired editor Chris Anderson told him. "That's because we have seen the dangers of technology first hand. I've seen it in myself. I don't want to see that happen to my kids…. This is rule No. 1: There are no screens in the bedroom. Period. Ever."

Exactly what those dangers are don't get much publicity from the tech sector. We will look at the research on that in the next chapter.

Evan Williams, co-founder of Blogger and Twitter

said that, instead of iPads, their two children have hundreds of books that they can pick up and read any time. "Yes, physical ones," added Bilton in his perplexity.

Steve Jobs' right-hand man at Apple, Jonathan Ive, revealed later that he sets very strict access rules for his twin boys. This isn't a Jobs peculiarity.

What did Steve Jobs's children do instead? They used to have dinner down a long table in the kitchen discussing books and history. Apparently.

So here's the question. If the people who shaped the IT revolution were so protective of their inventions when it came to their children, then why aren't more of us? Or is it right that those parents who are uncomfortable with the addiction to screens should feel so isolated? How come there is a sense that reality has shifted, so that – when it is online it feels more real than when it is now? How come so many children, increasingly young, live their lives online – and does it matter?

The author of the interview with Kitty the New York bartender (see front of this chapter), Emily Nussbaum, suggests that her transparency may simply be a response to the understanding by young people that privacy is effectively dead anyway. Every time we swipe our debit cards, or pass a security camera our lives are recorded. Every time we go through airport security, we pass machines where operators look at us through our clothing and record our nakedness. There is no privacy – so why pretend otherwise, or so they might reasonably say.

"So it may be time to consider the possibility that young people who behave as if privacy doesn't exist are actually the sane people, not the insane ones" she writes. "For someone like me, who grew up sealing my diary with a literal lock, this may be tough to accept. But under current circumstances, a defiant belief in holding things close to your chest might not be high-minded. It might be an artefact—quaint and naïve, like a determined faith that virginity keeps ladies pure..."

On the other hand, it is possible that the need to conduct your whole life online – under the unemotional and objective gaze of anybody who might be watching – may also be a symptom of the effect of gazing at screens yourself for too long. It may be what happens when you have watched too many Big Brother-style reality TV series. It may be that you have imbibed other people's intimate details, or peered too closely at the websites that reveal underarm hair on the most perfect celebrities.

Maybe that's what the prevailing online world does to its devotees. Maybe there are, as some experts believe, "real neurological changes involved".

We don't know, of course – and we are unlikely to know for certain. What we do propose is that, given the unease so many people feel about these issues, they need to be more openly discussed.

That is where this book comes in. There is so much available about the immediate and obvious dangers of the internet for children – sexual grooming, bullying, pornography and a great deal besides – but very little in comparison about how to police the amount of time they spend in front of screens, and whether it matters. This book tries to find out what families do in the UK – and we are aware that many don't even try – and what seems to work best. We look at the latest research and draw some conclusions.

We also try to keep an open mind for as long as possible. But we are aware that there are parents out there who feel completely alone – and are forced to accept that the online world is a fact, and accept that there is no intelligence at the heart of it, no benign authority figure at the controls (try reporting online abuse to Youtube, one of those vacant corporations where nobody is at home, and you will receive back the empty, helpless silence we have come to expect).

We know we are open to the accusation that we assume our children should be different to the other (perhaps) two thirds whose parents don't worry about screen time, or how much we spend on computer gaming kit. But we are also aware that we are assuming, as the middle classes tend to assume, that the government is at least vaguely on our side, shares our values, wants to support us to bring up our children in the best way that we can – when, actually, nothing could be further from the truth.

The government is actually firmly on the side of the screen pushers. The school system is dedicated to buying and pushing more Apple iPads. The truth is that Whitehall isn't interesting in our family life. They appear to want our children to be entirely open to whatever sells more stuff.

So where does that leave us? It leaves us with a worrying sense that we are out of step with mainstream life, different from our neighbours, unsure how to judge our children's screen time and finding it hard to police – and very unclear what to do.

That is why we wrote this short book. We may not be able to answer these questions definitively, but the purpose is to try and set them out more clearly – to set out the knowledge that is out there and list some of the strategies that other parents have used. We hope that the whole experience will turn out to be useful and even, dare we say, empowering.

The next chapter sets out what we can discover about the latest research and tries to draw some conclusions.

Then we look much more closely at the key issue, it seems to us, children's boredom – whether it matters, what it means and whether the online world makes it better or worse.

Then in Chapter IV we look at some of the different approaches used by the parents we interviewed. Finally, in Chapter V, we set out our ten strategies and try to explain them.

*"Gave into my child wanting a mobile phone in year
6. Earlier than we'd planned but she was the last in
her year to get one despite being the oldest. The texts
she would get - sometimes dozens of them on various
group things was overwhelming and the pressure to
join in and text back was huge - more texts saying
"why haven't you responded? Why aren't you my
friend anymore? Don't you like me?' when she had not
replied after just a few minutes. It was stressful and
she felt obliged to spend a lot of time on her phone
- this very quickly went from enjoyable to upsetting/
bewildering for her. In the end we banned her from
these group texts and she deleted all phone numbers
off her phone except for a small group of very close
friends. I texted round a few mothers to say that we
were doing this and why to try to limit any social fall
out. Several parents also went down the same route."*
Anonymous anecdote, posted online

When the Jobs family attitude to exposing their
children to the online world became clear in the UK,
and Ofcom – the telephone regulator – organised a
survey which revealed that seven in ten five to fifteen-
year-olds have access to tablet computers, with just
over a third owning their own, there was a brief flurry
of interest in what the UK tech gurus did.

Jonathan Taylor of Mind Candy described 'loose rules': "At weekends, my son can play computer games as long as he's done his homework, but a lot of times, his homework involves screen time, too."

Former Microsoft and Intel marketing manager Pierre Laurent sends his children to Steiner schools, which bans online involvement until the age of twelve. He described how internet companies deliberately set out to keep the attention of children hooked in to them:

> "It stops them discovering the world with
> their senses. And there's a risk to attention.
> It's not scientifically proven yet, but there's
> an idea that attention is like a muscle that
> we build. It's about being able to tune out
> all the distraction and focus on one thing.
> When you engage with these devices, you
> don't build that capacity. It's computer-aided
> attention; you're not learning to do it."

Finally, Anne Wojcicki, co-founder and CEO of gene-testing startup 23andme, also sets limits: "I don't get a thrill out of seeing my kids using tech... I much prefer when they get wonder out of picking strawberries in the garden. That said, I do love that my son texts me with fun uses for emoticons."

The truth is that it is the reservations of the tech pioneers that get the publicity. Their enthusiasm for technology is predictable and you quickly find that they are mainly divided, not between each other, but in their own minds – and quite rightly: there are few people who can see no advantages at all from IT. On the other hand, there is a sizeable group of people who worry that Americans now spend half their lives in front of screens.

The problem for parents is that they feel so alone. All truth is bound up in internet search engines, but the real truth is that it tends to reflect our own concerns back at us. If we are worried about an issue, then we will often find it all over the internet; if we are peculiar in our worries – or obscure for some reason – then we won't. That's just the way it is.

So if you want to find out about our prevailing nervousness about our children, especially when they go online, you'll find it immediately on the internet. Type the words 'children' and 'internet' into Google and what you find is overwhelming: it is all about internet safety, guarding children from violence, sexuality or online molesters.

We would not, of course, want to suggest that these are unimportant. But this book is about something else – the nervousness with which a minority (and it is probably only a minority) of people approach the time their children want to spend online, on games or Facebook or other social media, often on smartphones.

The reason we know this remains a minority concern is partly what we see around us – children of twelve or younger spending hours at a time, often into the night, playing games online. As far as we can tell, most parents are not worried about this. Most children – as our own children tell us incessantly – have access to the most sophisticated online games and gaming and computer or phone equipment.

The other reason is the research by Action for Children, published early in 2016, which showed that just under a quarter of parents (23 per cent) were worried about the amount of conflict with their children over the time spent online. That made it the biggest source of arguments in the home, over bedtimes, over homework and all the other potential flashpoints of family life. It is important. A quarter of the children in these age brackets – six to sixteen – are involved in these conflicts, so it is important that someone should look more closely at the issue, when the vast amount of news coverage does little more than spout statistics. And that is little help at all.

How many parents are we talking about here who feel uncomfortable about their children's screentime – not because of the immediate dangers but because of other fears? The research by Action for Children suggests that the unease is something that bothers 23.1 per cent of parents, and that they find it easier to get their children to do homework, go to bed or have a bath than turn off their phones, laptops and TVs. The next biggest struggle was persuading them to go to bed, but compared to screen time, only ten per cent found it hard to get them to do their homework, and less than five per cent wrestled with getting their offspring to have a bath.

It is clearly a source of friction for enough parents – around a quarter – for this to be worth discussing further. But let us be clear: this is not a guide book to the immediate dangers faced by children online: it is not about sexual predators or online bullying or sex and violence online. There are many places you can find out about that. It is about the time spent and the effects that might have on children.

Are iPads just the new TV?

First, let's look at the other point of view. There are certainly parents in the UK – perhaps even three quarters of them – who don't worry about these aspects of the risk to their children. It is worth asking in stark terms: how dare we cut children off from what is sometimes called kid's culture, as mediated by Rupert Murdoch and his media mogul equivalents?

What makes us think it is right to limit the interaction they may be having with their friends?

Our own generation also watched television a very great deal, and probably more than our children do. That was also a source of concern among our parents' generation, and much tut-tutting and disapproval – though perhaps little action. Before we give ourselves over to panic, it is worth just considering whether screen time and internet use isn't just the latest twist of the generation gap.

The new media professor at New York University, Clay Shirky, has a theory about this. "Whenever young people are allowed to indulge in something old people are not allowed to, it makes us bitter. What did we have? The mall and the parking lot of the 7-Eleven? It sucked to grow up when we did! And we're mad about it now."

Shirky says that we tend to feel that our approach to these matters is all about morality. The TV ratings company Nielsen's US figures suggest that children watch around 24 hours of television a week, compared to 28 hours in the mid-1970s when we were being brought up.

The real impact is also perhaps the kind of TV watched rather than the amount – there is certainly research evidence suggesting that this is the case. That implies perhaps that it is the kind of online activity that matters most, not the amount. Certainly, if we believe that education can civilise then we have to also believe that too much Grand Theft Auto can brutalise.

It is just that we have to guard ourselves against the suspicion that we are becoming a cliché of middle class concern, aware that we spend more time policing our children's screen time than almost anything else, pouring in a lifetime's resources in energy and angst and negotiating skills. We have to consider whether the sanest approach would be to let go a little, aware that they are at least learning computer skills and hand-eye co-ordination of a kind (though tennis can also give you that).

Perhaps we should laugh off the pre-teen humour of some of the Youtube stars - Yogscast spring to mind: people from Bristol who swear rather more than they would if they realised most of their viewers were eleven, and who think blowing things up is the apogee of humour. We used to watch Crackerjack after all. It didn't do much for our love of culture.

Other parents believe that technology and gadgets are essential for a child's development. This has to be true too, though the issue is about how much (an Ofcom survey showed that 12-15 year-olds were watching three and a half hours online than they were watching television).

A survey conducted for the clothing company Vertbaudet found that as many as four out of five parents believe technology is essential for a child. They found that 37 per cent of parents said that their child spent between one and two hours a day playing with tech gadgets, and 28 per cent said between two- and three hours. They also found that 38 per cent of two- to five-year-olds own an Android tablet, and 32 per cent own an iPad. Almost a third of them also have a mobile phone.

Even more (35%) say that they use IT to entertain their children (the same as use television for the same): about 85 per cent of mothers say they do this so they can get on with something else. In that respect, the high use of screens may just be a reflection of how busy people are, of high rents and high mortgages, which keep people out of the home juggling childcare. This is not a condemnation. Quite the reverse.

So what is the problem? The answer is that there are a range of issues people talk about and worry about. These are the main ones.

1. Screens may make children stupid

Recent research by a team at Cambridge University suggests that parents might have some reason to worry about this. They found that an extra hour a day of television, internet or computer game time in Year 10 was linked to poorer grades at GCSE. They had recorded the activities of more than 800 fourteen-year-olds. When they analysed their GCSE results at sixteen, they found those who had spent an extra hour a day on screens saw a fall in results equivalent to two grades overall.

What the study failed to show, as so often with this kind of research, was why this was. The obvious suggestion is that it might mean children arriving at school tired after spending time in front of a screen late at night.

The odd thing about the Cambridge research was that the effect on GCSE grades happened even if they worked hard at school work. Even if pupils spent more time studying, more time spent watching TV or online still harmed their results, the analysis suggested. Extra time on moderate to vigorous physical activity had no effect on academic achievement.

2. Screens may make our children fat

One recent survey suggested that children spend on average around 17 hours a week in front of a screen – almost double the 8.8 weekly hours spent playing outside. This is a low estimate: a 2007 survey in the USA suggested that children between eight and eighteen spent on average 44.5 hours per week in front of screens. That is unlikely to be less now, but it was a decade ago. If it is still true, that is more than an adult working week.

3. Screens may get them into the habit of suppressing their feelings

If there is something addictive about the internet, and online games in particular – even the milder ones like Minecraft – it could be because children can bypass the things that worry them on an almost permanent basis. They can slip out of painful feelings and into a comfortable online world that they have created.

This could be related to the one-dimensional interaction they get online. One study found that girls spend more time than boys on social media sites, but they were still not interacting with real people, face to face, which is when they really learn. As the child psychologist Michele Elliott, said:

> "When children are using these devices
> they are not communicating or interacting
> with anyone else. They may be very good
> at texting but how do they do when they
> have to meet someone face to face?"

This may be simply a reflection of one of the reasons society faces such a depression problem – it suggests that plugging into music or screens or other devices all the time prevents us from processing and dealing with feelings. Freud said that all he could do was to change despair into "ordinary human misery". The suggestion here is that too much screentime prevents this natural process from happening.

4. Screens may drive out other kinds of activity.

The current generation of children in most Western societies spends more time in front of a screen than any before it. A study back in 2010 – before even the phenomenal rise of Apple's iPad and other tablets – estimated that by the age of ten, children had access to an average of five screens in their lives. That number, the psychologist Aric Sigman suggests, has almost certainly risen since.

As well as the main family TV, for example, many young children have their own bedroom telly along with portable computer game consoles, smartphone, family computer and a laptop and tablet computer. By the age of seven, the average child will have spent a full year of 24-hour days watching recreational screen media, said Sigman. In fact, over the course of childhood, children spend more time watching screens than they spend in school.

It is worth noting that, given the high point of television watching a generation ago, this has actually been true for some time.

5. Screens may not help children develop.

In 2013, the US Department of Health recommended that children aged under two should not be in front of a screen at all, and over that age the maximum leisure screen time should be no more than two hours a day. The French government has even banned digital terrestrial TV aimed at all children under three, while Australia and Canada have similar recommendations and guidelines.

The Harvard clinical psychologist Catherine Steiner-Adair has argued that a baby's brain is hardwired to learn language, emotions and how to regulate them. She says there is no productive role that technology can play in the life of a baby under two years. That is why parents in Taiwan are obliged by law to monitor their children's screen time, and face fines if they are spending too much time in front of them. Needless to say, the UK government has no medical or governmental guidelines on screen time.

Steiner-Adair found that babies showed signs of distress when they looked to a parent for a reassuring connection and discovered the parent is distracted by technology. In fact, she found that 70 percent of kids think their parents spend too much time on devices, and accuse their parents of double standards.

There are also implications about addiction. Like other addictions, screen time releases the neurotransmitter dopamine (see more in next chapter). "There are concerns among neuro-scientists that this dopamine being produced every single day for many years – through for example playing computer games – may change the reward circuitry in a child's brain and make them more dependent on screen media," said Sigman

6. Screens can cut them off from social interaction.
There is controversial research, again involving Sigman, about whether screen time drives out face-to-face contact. This matters when a lack of social connection is associated with physiological changes and an increased incidence of illness. In fact, the latest medical research suggests that having no friends is as dangerous to your health as smoking.

7. It may affect the ability to concentrate and relax.
Catherine Steiner-Adair's book The Big Disconnect is sceptical about whether children actually learn to do two or three things at the same time. She says that children who use screens a great deal may become adept at multi-tasking, but lose the ability to focus on what is most important. You need that to be good at problem-solving later.

Part of this is that screens mimic daylight and a few minutes of screen stimulation can delay melatonin release by several hours. That can lead to children not getting enough sleep. Research into animal behaviour suggests that screen light can lead to depression.

8. It may make children aggressive or grumpy.
This one goes to the heart of the debate. Many parents believe that battering or shooting enemies every day on screen is bound to seep into attitudes and behaviour. Others echo their children who say that there is no connection – they are perfectly able to distinguish illusion and reality. The jury remains out. It probably depends on the child.

Most parents can think of ways that computer games seem to lead to irritability in their kids, or even rages. There does seem to be a record of agitation and, conversely, also exhaustion linked to online gaming. There have been suggestions that these abnormal levels of arousal can be linked to an inability to relate to other people, and it can lead to a cycle of treatment for depression or ADHD, which is a serious business and not necessarily successful. Again, more on this in the next chapter.

There are links to other reasons here. Because the children are mentally exhausted, rage can give them injections of energy.

The pros and cons of electronic fasting
This is how Dr Victoria Dunkley suggested the idea in *Psychology Today*:

"Both parents and clinicians may be 'barking up the wrong tree'. That is, they're trying to treat what looks like a textbook case of mental disorder, but failing to rule out and address the most common environmental cause of such symptoms—everyday use of electronics. Time and again, I've realised that regardless of whether there exists any 'true' underlying diagnoses, successfully treating a child with mood dysregulation today requires methodically eliminating all electronics use for several weeks— an 'electronics fast' – to allow the nervous system to reset. If done correctly, this intervention can produce deeper sleep, a brighter and more even mood, better focus and organisation, and an increase in physical activity. The ability to tolerate stress improves, so meltdowns diminish in both frequency and severity. The child begins to enjoy the things they used to, is more drawn to nature, and imaginary or creative play returns. In teens and young adults, an increase in self-directed behaviour is observed—the exact opposite of apathy and hopelessness."

Dr Dunkley suggests that, "After the fast, once the brain is reset, the parent can carefully determine how much if any electronics use the child can tolerate without symptoms returning".

The trouble is that, for most parents and most children, this kind of fast requires a huge commitment in time and energy and mental strength to get through the conflict. Of course, if your child is seriously ill then that goes without saying that you will make it your first priority. But otherwise, the explosion of rage that is likely to follow seems unnecessary to endure. Why should we confront it, we tell ourselves? OK, our children are acting as if they have been captured by Apple or Microsoft, and their brains removed for reprogramming, but why should we confront it alone – unless the problems are obvious and difficult.

Part of the difficulty is that we have been given no yardsticks to help us decide how serious our children's addiction is, and hence how urgently we need to address it.

It hardly needs saying that this leaves parents confused and without much support, certainly not from the government or the education system who have appeared to swallow the blandishments of the online world themselves.

For those who worry about time spent online, the Americans (in this case the Center for Internet

Addiction Recovery) have set out a series of warning signs for worried parents to search for if they want to decide whether their children have pathological internet use.

Do they lose track of time while online? (everyone does that, I believe). Do they sacrifice hours of sleep to spend time online? Do they get agitated or angry when online time is interrupted (this seems to us only natural)? Do they check email or phones several times a day (everyone does)? Do they get irritable if not allowed access to the internet? Do they spend time online in place of homework or chores or instead of being with friends or family? Do they disobey time limits that have been set for internet usage or lie about the amount of time they are spending online or sneak online when no one is around?

The trouble with this list is that it probably applies to most children with a passing interest in the online world. It certainly applies to ours, and to us. And if it applies to everyone it is undoubtedly scaremongering. In fact, the problem for parents who worry about this issue is that they then become subject to all the weaknesses of the internet too. They can't get unbiased information, some of the information is deeply untrustworthy, and it is very hard to access any help.

The other problem is that it gives you no

instructions about what to do about it when the world about you appears to have gone insane. It may be that the electronic fast is a useful solution if necessary, but it has to be done when the children are young enough to benefit, and perhaps later with some consent.

Otherwise, we suggest our ten-point strategy at the end of this book.

Don't forget to chill

It isn't difficult to scare ourselves about the problems of online addiction, especially if we are – come on, admit it – just a little bit addicted ourselves. We probably survived very heavy television use when we were children, and – although this is a step-change – it will not help to problematise our children because they enjoy going online.

That is not to say we should do nothing as parents. The Education Policy Institute recently found that a third of the fifteen-year-olds in the UK were what they called 'extreme internet users', which the OECD defines as more than six hours a day on a non-school day. It includes television time, with more than half spending three hours or more a day on social media.

They also put the research in more context, unsure whether the online time undermines mental health or whether those with depression find themselves online more. We were surprised about that – the cause or effect question really does have to be answered better than that.

But perhaps we were most surprised about the Institute's conclusion: that parents should not control time online because it prevents children getting the skills they need to stay safe, and emotional skills in particular.

Does it really require three hours practice a day to stay safe on social media? We doubt it. We also doubt the emotional lessons, apart from rather brutal ones, that can be learned fully online – that seems to imply the usual official muddle about the difference between the online and real worlds.

Yes, some of your real friends may also be Facebook friends, but real friendship is not mediated online. You do not learn how to deal with people except by meeting them face to face. Sorry, but it is true. We believe that is the rule which should govern the rest.

But we were not satisfied by this brief overview of the research. Something else seemed to us to be more important. That is why we looked more closely at the phenomenon of boredom.

"It wasn't always like this: until a couple of years ago, rather than gawping at Youtubers drinking live goldfish and who knows what else they get up to, my darling boy wasted his waking hours playing games, specifically Mine-bloody-craft. How I hated it, with its stupid, make-believe world of pixellated, Lego-faced critters and monsters. Some commentators went so far as to argue that a Minecraft habit was somehow educational and healthy, the fools..."
Bon Granleese, The Guardian, 7 Jan 2016

Readers deserve to know a little about where the authors of this short book are coming from in this debate, given that our basic attitudes towards technology are bound to colour our attitudes to the way our children use it. Also, if all you read was the previous chapter about some of the broad research that has been carried out over the past decade, you might be forgiven for wondering whether we were disguised Luddites, crusading against new technology.

One of us will admit to a conservatism that perhaps should be set aside in this respect. Because there is no doubt that IT has huge benefits for both communication and learning, and that the computer skills that online games and social media provide for young people will be important in their lives.

We are sceptical about the cod psychology that suggests children learn motor skills from online games which they can't perfectly well get from playing football or table tennis in the outside world. But there are skills in finding information online, and at understanding the new kinds of logic which will clearly help them later, if they can master it.

We are also aware of the great psychologist James Hillman's suggestion that children sometimes need to react against their parents' constraints to find their role in life. It means that simply letting your children decide everything may not be as useful as it seems to the liberal-minded. We parents are bound to get things wrong sometimes, and it maybe that our mistakes form part of their impetus for finding their genius in the online world, despite us rather than because of us.

Generation Facebook

"When you're talking about technology and you're old, it's such a cliché – that's what people were worrying about in 2006. I would say that at university FB makes sense as it's the perfect tool for university life – because that's what it was built for by Zuckerberg. It's to make

sure that all your friends are going to the same place, and it's cheap/free to advertise – it works exactly as it should do, as a way of linking up; it complements a time of intense social life. What I don't understand is why people over – or under – a certain age would use it."
Freya, 19-year old student

Writing as parents, not experts

The message of this book is that, as parents, we have to act, make decisions, wrestle with the issues – rather than assuming that they will emerge from our inaction. That does not, of course, mean that we have all the answers. Parents rarely do – they are engaged in a kind of offline game themselves, learning and making mistakes and learning again. And it is as parents, writing for other parents – and emphatically not as experts – that we have shaped this book.

There are other implications from all this. The conclusion of this book therefore cannot be total abstinence from the online world, any more than it is likely to be a starry-eyed and naïve belief. The online world is important in our lives, and it provides a bizarrely large chunk of conversation among our children's friends. They will have to learn to navigate safely there but you don't learn to navigate in the world by staying indoors.

A generational divide

> One in five young people, according to a recent public health report, secretly turn on their phones under the covers at night to check on updates. Many prefer to watch, comment and share the YouTube videos of strangers they identify with rather than speak to someone at school about a problem. Adults need to understand that for today's children, online spaces are not a distraction but a place where they enact real-world relationships and experiment with who they are.
> Financial Times, 13 June 2017

As we will see in the next chapter, the varied approaches that many parents take to the issue, no matter what they believe about new technology, are actually quite similar.

As we explained, we both have children ourselves – one has girls and the other has boys, which present different challenges. The boys in particular provided the spark to the book, though we will not be writing about them in particular.

We are aware of another family where, in separate incidents of rage over a 36-hour period, one child broke an alarm clock and the other a laptop – in both cases, the incidents were linked to computer games. In one case, the rage emerged from not being allowed to go online before school. In the other, it was a general, and quite understandable rage of frustration with the way one child was being treated online.

It did strike us, when we heard this story, that there must be a better way and it is frustrating for parents who feel that there is so little help or advice available. This is another returning theme in this book – that most professional or official support is available is mainly about force-feeding the more vulnerable children with technology, and encouraging them to spend increasing amounts of time online and not outside, or reading, or any of the other activities that might serve them best in later life.

That in itself is a disputed idea and a controversial sentence and it is beyond the scope of this book. The main reason we began to wonder more challengingly about the received wisdom about time spent online was not so much the rage, but its opposite: boredom.

Yes, boys in particular seem angrier when they are online or have just been online. Their aggression levels seem higher, which is perhaps not surprising since they have been immersed in an online world which is often red in tooth, claw and rocket launcher, and where they are encouraged to earn points by bludgeoning to death passing furry creatures. But at other times, and especially when they have spent more time online, children seem to be even more prone to boredom than usual.

Getting bored online

So here is the hypothesis. It may be that spending too much time on online games or on social media makes children bored.

This is an unexpected and paradoxical idea and it seems to have been very little researched. So let us be precise about what we mean. We argue that there is a link, which we see in practice, between online gaming and boredom, because immersion in this perfect, controllable and shiny world makes the real world seem tawdry and dull.

Since this is often what adolescents feel about their own family or their own home town, that they are dull reflections of the world beyond home, you can see how the online world of games and social media gets mixed up with the business of adolescent frustration. You can then see how the effect of increased immersion into the fantasy world of online gaming seems to make them more bored than usual with mundane reality – and with less shiny activities.

It may even increase their confusion about the boundaries between real and virtual – a generational obsession – just as those children who spend too much time on social media via mobile phones can find it hard sometimes to distinguish between real friends and the Facebook kind.

Social media platforms and mental health

A survey of 1,500 young people across the UK, the Royal Society for Public Health found that heavy use of platforms such as Instagram, Snapchat, Facebook, Twitter and YouTube stoked anxiety, depression and poor sleep in children. One recommendation was to introduce a pop-up 'heavy usage' warning; if young people used social media for two or more hours a day, there was a correlation with an increased rate of anxiety and depression. Financial Times, 13 June 2017

Different children react in very different ways. "Comparing my two daughters' use of social media is like night and day," says Linda, a mother of three (two girls, one boy):

"The older one is very scared of it but uses Facebook for making arrangements. The younger one is on her phone from the minute she gets up until she goes to sleep; most of the time she's

interacting with a close group of friends so I can
see that it's a tool for extending time spent with
genuine friends. As an only child who suffered
socially, I'm biased in seeing it as a good thing.
The only time it bothers me with her is when
I want her to experience something with me,
like watching a film and seeing her reactions to
it – I feel she's only ever 75 per cent with me
as she always has her phone with her. My son
mainly seems to use social media for arguments,
having slanging matches on Instagram."

It may not be helpful, therefore, to generalise about the different ways that children use social media, often partly to keep sane in a less than sane world.

Research from the Royal Society of Public Health (RSPH) found that heavy users of Snapchat and Instagram were not just using them to reach out to friends, but to explore their identity — including sexuality and body image. Social media platforms had a very positive impact on allowing kids to express themselves and form an identity. For example, one gender-fluid 14-year-old found that Instagram was the place that helped them find a supportive community. Two girls diagnosed with anorexia as young teenagers used Instagram to document their recovery process and connect to other kids with similar problems.

On the flip side, many of the kids surveyed by the RSPH also rated Instagram as the platform with the most negative impact on body image. A major issue that came out of the study was problems around body image. through viewing curated or heavily filtered images that are not necessarily proper representations of reality. There was also a gender split, especially with Instagram: girls expressed a massively more negative perception of how it affected their body image than boys did.

Should we worry about gaming addiction?

This clash between real and fantasy remains a hypothesis. But it is supported by a teacher called Tom Chatfield who described himself as a recovering gaming addict and wrote about it in the Guardian, interviewing another one. The younger former addict was called Daniel – then 24 – who described his life at the age of 15:

> "*I would say I was playing 15 hours a day at the peak. I kind of half block it out because I hated school so much but the worst year I can remember was when*
> *I was playing EverQuest. I was 16, and I was getting up at two in the morning and*

going downstairs on to my mum's laptop
to play. I was up until eight, and then I'd
get back into bed saying I was ill."

EverQuest was an interesting phenomenon, at one stage rivalling Russia's per head of GDP in the late 1990s, because of how much of its fantasy currency was being manufactured by semi-slaves in Chinese warehouses. It was a parallel world, sort of Dungeons and Dragons and McDonalds all rolled into one, where corporates had also set themselves up with virtual presences. It no longer rivals Russia's GDP per head, but it retains some of its addictive fascination.

The business of playing truant to stay in the gaming world ought to be a side issue because it will not affect the vast majority of families. But in 2011, another teacher, Richard Gribble, from Plymouth, carried out a survey in his ordinary school class of children aged ten or eleven. He found that over three quarters of them were playing video games every night, and over a third were playing in the mornings as well. Some were staying up until 4am to play, others waking up at 5am before school. Some were falling asleep in class, which was hardly surprising.

How common is this kind of extreme behaviour? It may be more common that you think. We all know children and teenagers who sneak off late at night to find their phone or early in the morning to play online. But then, a great deal of the business of gaming goes on behind closed doors and below the radar. Since 2008, the gaming industry has been the biggest entertainment sector in the world, bigger than either films or music.

The following year, the game Modern Warfare 2 – part of the Call of Duty series which mimics street fighters – was the biggest seller on Amazon, bigger than the final Harry Potter film which came out the same year. Yet the coverage and attention it gets remains minimal.

This is how Tom Chatfield explained the appeal:

"Part of what makes games, and online games in particular, so much more appealing than other media is the fact they are potentially infinite time sinks. Once enthralled by a game we may stay that way for weeks, months, or even years. An online world is a real-life never-ending story, with the player as the protagonist. There is no happily ever after. The only real time limit is the need for the player to eat and sleep, and, in the most extreme cases, even those are ignored."

This explains a little how a thirty-year-old man from China died after a three-day gaming spree, during which he had barely eaten or slept.

How many gamers are addicted?

There are some authorities who suggest it may be as high as eight per cent. Mark Griffiths, director of the International Gaming Research Unit at Nottingham University puts the figure at less than half of one per cent. But this is because he defines 'addiction' extremely narrowly, covering people who are unable to stop playing despite the damage done to partners, children or relationships.

He may be right, but that is not to ignore the addictive elements. The truth is that encouragement for at least mild addictions are built into the games – the drive to hook you in and keep you there by the manipulation of points, levels and peer pressure.

But there are still worrying parallels with alcohol and drug addictions because the same parts of people's brains are stimulated when they are playing these games, often perhaps because they are symptoms of problems that children have with self-esteem or relationships with their parents. As if any child was immune to that.

Aggression-boredom

You might make parallel remarks about mobile phones, which are – or at least they seem to be – a conduit to a world of popularity and adult experience, or a world of Youtube videos where parents don't go and don't understand and where people find it exciting or funny to use the word 'fuck' for emphasis – but appear unaware that most of their viewers are actually eleven.

But it was in Tom's article that we found some confirmation of what I had feared about the aggression-boredom influence of gaming. A mother of a sixteen-year-old who has been gaming since the age of six but had recently taken up with playing Modern Warfare 2 with friends online.

"We have episodes of violence," she said about her son. "He threatened to push me down the stairs, which is very unlike him. He's probably the nicest lad you could meet when he's not playing the game. He really has just become paralysed. You can't even have a conversation with him if it's not about the game."

She looked for help and was turned away by social services, doctors and even the police. She was rebuffed at every turn. She described the world of gaming addiction as "quite an isolated world, without the help". As indeed it is.

Adrenaline and self-reg

Most of us are not gaming addicts, nor Facebook addicts. Most of our children are not either. But there are still issues that need to be tackled.

The propensity for addiction, the physiological reaction and the stress goes some way to confirming the behavior of some of the children we know – the rage when denied the habit of creeping out late at night or in the early hours of the morning to play. But what about the boredom?

Well, this is where it gets interesting. There are studies which show that there is a link between boredom and over-stimulating the brain. The American psychiatrist Stuart Shankar, whose book Self-Reg is all about how to calm children down, argues that online games produce adrenaline which force children to dip into their reserves of energy. This in turn produces the stress hormone cortisol. Boredom, says Dr Shankar, is simply the unpleasant sensation of having too much cortisol in the bloodstream. When the stimulation stops, childrens' brains swing between higher and lower levels of arousal.

Back in the 1990s, scientists found that online games could double the level of dopamine in the bloodstream, which is the addiction hormone which gives people a temporary high. When children start to come down again, they go into a state of anxiety where they search out another high. That explains the feeling of boredom. "Violence – themed role playing or first-person-shooter games are habituating children to a heightened level of arousal that renders more sedate games not just boring but even unpleasant," wrote Dr Shankar in Self-Reg.

Shankar emphasises the importance, not of making the sources of addiction inaccessible, but of encouraging children to see the links to the triggers for their mood swings for themselves. Shankar's approach is a biochemical reaction to a psychological phenomenon, but it does provide an explanation for the underlying chemistry. It is also a heavy-handed approach, because most of our children are not hooked on anything seriously. The issue is boredom and why it is that children are so frightened of it when it begins to seep in again – and whether the online cure to boredom is worse than the disease (evidence from the USA suggests that heavy internet use makes you two and a half times more likely to be depressed).

Boredom played such an important role in the lives of adults and children in previous generations. Jane Austen's heroines were bored out of their wits for most of the time. Why the terror of boredom now?

A breath of fresh thinking

To find out more about the link between boredom, online gaming and social media, we contacted Teresa Belton, a visiting fellow in the School of Education and Lifelong Learning at the University East Anglia, who had stumbled into the field as a result of researching the effects of television on children's imagination in the 1990s.

Teresa said she had restricted the time and type of her own children's viewing when they were young, on the basis of gut feeling. She had also been involved in a small charity called 'Play for Life' which tried to develop alternatives to playing with 'war toys'. "We began to ask, if war toys are bad because they implicitly endorse the idea it's OK to kill or maim people, then what is good play like?" she told me. "The aim was to encourage fresh thinking amongst parents about what kinds of free-time activities help children's emotional, social, cultural and spiritual development."

That led her to undertake her own doctoral research into the influence of television and videos on children's imagination. To do this, she looked at the stories written by all the ten- to-twelve-year-old pupils in five assorted schools over a term.

The school where she piloted her approach had just got their Year 6 children to write a story called 'The Face at the Window'. The ninety stories showed a "marked degree of crime and violence," said Teresa. But then, the title was rather sinister. To test whether it was the title or the influence of violent screen material that had prompted the crime and violence in these stories, she set another story task, with the title 'By the Light of the Candle'. This time, crime and violence took a back seat.

Teresa made another overall observation; many of the stories were actually rather dull. To investigate the influence of the screen on the imaginativeness of the story-making, she chose twelve children whose story apparently had no connection with screen content, twelve whose narrative was fundamentally dependent on screen material, and twelve in whose tale there was a passing reference, and studied these children in some depth, with interviews, exercises for the imagination and oral story-telling in addition.

"My conclusion was that there was actually much less active influence from the screen than I expected to find," says Teresa. "The principal input came from the children's own direct experience, be it social, physical, emotional or cultural. The screen did sometimes stimulate imitative imaginative, but only in a few children did it stimulate transformative imagination which could turn the screen images and ideas into something new."

Teresa was struck by the sheer lack of imagination in many of the stories she read. Then she found a number of earlier academic studies, undertaken while television was first coming in, which had all concluded that television had a stifling effect on children's imaginative capacities.

How much boredom should we give them?

Teresa Belton published an article in an academic journal, which tried to find an explanation for these findings, and quoted the American psychologist and educationist Jerome Bruner, who said that boredom in small doses is stimulating, but in large doses could be destructive.

The significance of boredom is that children (indeed adults too) often fall back on television or a digital device, to keep boredom at bay.

"The apparent stifling effect of watching TV on imagination is a concern, as imagination is important," she wrote later. "Not only does it enrich personal experience, it is also necessary for empathy – imagining ourselves in someone else's shoes – and is indispensable in creating change."

That would have been that, except that the editors of the journal sent a copy of the article to a Sunday Times journalist who built it into a piece with the eye-catching title, 'Researcher tells parents boredom is good for their children'.

Following up the explosion of interest the article created led Teresa more recently to interview four people in the public eye who had mentioned the creative potential of their own boredom – the artist Grayson Perry, the writer and actress Meera Syal, the poet Felix Dennis, and the neuro-scientist Professor Susan Greenfield. They talked to her about how creativity often involves going into yourself; turning over ideas and trying different approaches, the stimulus provided by limited resources, and how having time to fill can push you to try all manner of new things. All rather at odds with the world of social media and computer games, which involve facing outwards towards the world, giving instant responses, always looking to make a good impression or the right move, and interacting only with a screen and with other people interacting with a screen.

The technological background has moved on since Teresa was carrying out her initial research. Children watch considerably less television, but probably spend more time in front of screens – encouraged now by schools. They are increasingly passive, or they seem to be. The crime rate has plummeted, along with teenage pregnancy as a result of young people being a bit less bored. So why do we feel that my children are rendered more bored by online games?

Is it because they are made less able to deal with boredom? Is it that ordinary life seems more mundane, and boredom more threatening, as a result? "It does ring very true," says Teresa. "Probably it has something to do with the fact that everything on the screen is instant. The screen responds instantly and the speed of the game is very fast, whereas the essence of boredom is the opposite:

> "It could also be that the screen dictates the
> terms of the way we use it, whereas activity in
> the real, unprogrammed world requires children
> to be able to take initiatives. So perhaps what
> children experience as boredom after playing
> online is actually a sense of disempowerment
> and a need to exercise their own agency
> and personal inventiveness; or a desire for
> something less complete, perfect, finite, and
> more spontaneous, organic and unfolding."

Nurturing creativity

To turn boredom into creativity, you need some inner resources, such as patience, persistence, and confidence that some idea or possibility will present itself, she says. For some activities you will also need space, which many people don't have – in this respect the great dilemma about the online world is partly a by-product of small homes, a dysfunctional housing market and toxic urban environments, but there is little that parents can do about this on their own.

What they can do is be a little more willing for their children to make a mess – with the requirement, too, that the children will clear up afterwards.

"A lot of people are afraid of their children making a mess," said Teresa. "There are usually very simple things around the home which can be used to develop the imagination and resourcefulness in play, but this kind of experimenting and exploring is not neat and tidy. We live in such a consumerist society now. People often think that you have to buy ready-made stuff in order to be constantly occupied. Neuroscientists are discovering how letting the mind wander, rather than focusing it all the time, is good for brain function and problem solving."

Teresa Belton says we need to help children achieve the state of 'flow', an idea pioneered by the Hungarian psychologist Mihaly Csikszentmihalyi, which we experience when we are so completely immersed in doing something that we don't notice time passing, and our abilities are stretched enough to keep us interested.

Now, we can't help noticing that children can achieve something along those lines in a successful online game. It does have to be right. A little too difficult, result: anxiety. Not difficult enough, result: boredom.

The question is how often online activity provides this sense of flow. Part of the problem is the extreme frustration when children meet technology. The other, more fundamental problem is that the games are too overwhelming. They allow no variation, no imagination, no tweaks; it all has to be done on their own limited terms – they are universes with constraints, built in such detail that they constrain the imagination too.

The problem is that the sensory experience is very limited, even on the biggest screens. It is two-dimensional however much it looks three-dimensional, and has very little practical value for navigating the real world.

It lures you in but has none of the sheer awkwardness of the authentic world. It can be hard for children to learn to value the irritations and the sheer cussedness of reality compared to the slick certainties of the online or social media world. But authentic is awkward, and as many adults as children sometimes fail to understand its importance and its pre-eminence (as if online communities really have any kind of equality with real ones).

Teresa Belton also says it is important that parents model in their own behaviour and attitudes the relationship with technology they want their children to develop:

> "*A good attention span is invaluable for all sorts of reasons, so constant distraction by phones is pretty unhealthy. There seems to be something compulsive about phone and computer use for most of us, so the older that children are when come into regular contact with digital media, the better it will be for them. If parents can bring themselves to limit their own reliance on their phone or the online world, and try to regard it as a tool to use for a particular purpose, they can show that the default mode is to be in the real world, and that there are times when they consciously choose to use computers for entertainment or information.*"

The antidote to boredom, as Teresa Belton writes in her book Happier People Healthier Planet, is green space, bits and pieces to make a mess with, and a sense of meaning and purpose.

This is no doubt true, but we were left wondering whether the over-reliance by children, parents and young people on online gaming and social media was a symptom or a cause of the loss of meaning and purpose. We assume thst it is a little of both.

IV | From tigers and negotiators to low-tech parents

"We were on holiday this summer with my brother in law and his tweens, and on day 2 a massive thunderstorm knocked out the wifi for a couple of days. Cue much wailing and gnashing of teeth for a few hours (and constant questions about when the technician was going to come), but after a while acceptance set in and lo and behold the tweens decided it was fun to hang out with us after all, go for walks, swims etc etc. Bliss was it in that dawn to be alive. And on the third day, the wifi came back on, and they returned to the Matrix..."
Online anecdote

We carried out a series of interviews with parents about how they deal with their childrens' online lives, not about their safety – which is beyond the scope of this book – but about the time they spend there. What we found was a wide variety of attitudes but a fascinating number of parallel conclusions that they come to.

THE RELAXED PARENT
Interview with parent of two boys (eldest is ten).

One of the biggest challenges for me is knowing how much screentime children should have. I'm not convinced that anybody knows and whether it's the same for every child. It's knowing how to find the balance between how much freedom or privacy to give them when they're using computers. Should they take their ipads off to their bedroom or should we be hovering over them because of undesirable websites? I feel very confused about it.

We had an internet safety talk at school where they asked us to forget about the technology and instead focus on your relationship with your children and keeping open lines of communication. The advice was not to think of the computer as anything different to any other part of their life that they can talk to you about. That did make things seem a bit less scary – although it felt as they were almost saying you've got no chance of staying ahead technically so just make sure you've got a good relationship with your child.

They gave us some really useful info – which I've filed and never looked at again... It's such a learning curve for parents as well as children – I'm just relying on keeping an eye on it!

Recently, my eldest son started his own Youtube channel, which we were very dubious about – it seemed like the big wide world encroaching. But the videos he's made where he talks to the camera about himself (about his brother, his fish, school) seemed to help him express himself really well, and in a way I've never heard him do so face-to-face.

He's quite shy but good at computers and his online persona was more confident than in the flesh. I've not sure if this is a good or a bad thing. He first made a video at a friend's house so he did learn about it from a real-life connection.

Both children fight over who has the main computer for certain games – each of them may have their own ipads but they screen-stack. They could be watching a video and skyping a friend on another device and playing a game if you let them.

They are also constantly lobbying for more time. Getting them away from their screens is such a flash point, that moment where you have to say: come off the computer because we're going out in 20 minutes and you have to get ready. There's something completely mesmerising or hypnotic about it – not just for children (I'm on a screen all day myself), but the problem is when it seems more exciting than anything else.

In the end we've found it easier to set quite strict boundaries rather than have daily battles during the week, so there's no computers before school or after school from Monday to Thursday. Unfortunately, it's beginning to get a bit blurred because of homework for the older one. I'm also happy if they're doing something useful and creative. My youngest is into his rock collection – he wanted to catalogue them by taking photos with his ipad, but when I came back a short time later he was playing a game, so it has to be intensively supervised.

We used to threaten to take screen time away if they misbehaved but they hated that and got really upset, saying that we were blackmailing them. Now we've switched that around to say they could earn screentime with good behaviour. This works quite well in that it's meant they've started doing chores, which they didn't do before.

Now they have to lay the table, keep their rooms tidy, and so on – we did have a ridiculously complex chart initially with time allocation for different tasks but they were clocking up about 14 hours a day! I think the system has helped on all fronts, both with improving general behaviour and to see screentime as a reward not a basic right.

I would describe us as quite hands-off or relaxed compared to a lot of people; I know some parents whose kids only get 30 minutes on Saturdays and Sundays. Although we're strict during the week, it's virtually unlimited at the weekend, although this can make it difficult to do other things – my eldest never wanted to do anything else, so we have scaled it down by organising other activities like playing tennis.

We did read a book that had a big influence on us – Calmer, Easier, Happier Parenting [by Noel Janis-Norton] – which shockingly recommended only one hour screentime a day (unless it's a special occasion like watching a film), so we obviously haven't followed it to the letter. We watch more than that ourselves so it's hard to expect children to do same. However, the book's philosophy about inducements reinforced what we were already doing.

Summary

- Allowing unlimited time at weekends but strict on weekdays.
- Using good behaviour for more online time maybe better than punishing bad behaviour with less.
- Starting a Youtube channel has helped with confidence.

The Techie Parent
Divorced father of a 12-year old son, David, who he has to stay every weekend.

Digital technology is entirely my life [as a computer programmer and translator], and I try to do stuff with David such as playing some of the computer games he likes with him.

As a divorced parent who has him to stay every

weekend, he does talk to me about the different regimes between his parents; he tells me 'you understand it, Daddy, and [his mum] doesn't, and she won't let me have more than 30 minutes a day.' I think I'm more flexible about it for a number of reasons, one of them being that I have installed security devices on his computer and phone that report on what sites he visits.

It sounds 'big-brother-esque', but it may help parents feel more relaxed, and things have been blocked that friends have sent him. Of course, there are still things to be alert about, some that you have to partly take on trust and also be around them generally to see how they're reacting to what they're doing online.

I'm also more likely to be with him when he's doing digital stuff than his mum is – and less likely to think tech is going to rot our brains. I would be more worried if he wanted to spend all his time using the stuff – but, at the moment, he seems genuinely happy to do alternative things to computers. Either that, or he's really good at acting, out of fear that everything could be taken off him!

Possibly, the way that David isn't here all the time distorts the picture – when he is at mine we really want to do stuff together. Most of the conflict over technology so far has been with his mum. A couple of times she's phoned me up to discuss issues, such as when she's found that – after he's played a game after dinner – that he can't get to sleep after, because of the adrenaline rush.

Normally, when David's here, he doesn't go to school the next day, but I initially agreed to implement the 30-minute limit as part of being consistent a couple of years ago. Now though I don't feel it's flexible enough so I sometimes fudge the issue, like when he has flu and wants to play games.

Educationally, being able to look up stuff on the internet is incredibly useful – I'd have known loads more as a kid if technology had been around. We don't use it to keep in touch during the week, but he does have a Youtube channel and makes videos that he posts there. I did have some initial misgivings but I have been impressed with him doing stop motion animation. It takes hours to do but seems like a positive way to focus on creating something that has definite challenges to produce and requires sustained attention.

I also think that playing computer games has made him more interested in doing things like coding at school. Coding is something that kids can learn as analytical thinking, a bit like maths.

On the whole, I think I'm very relaxed about things – I characterise my parenting style around tech the same as I do any other aspect of parenting, loving but with boundaries. Of course, it hasn't been difficult so far and it's not something we discuss that often – but I appreciate that the teenage years may bring fresh challenges and that it's a different dynamic with a dad who's not with him all the time!

Summary
- **Using technology to check online time and safety.**
- **Limiting time, a little reluctantly, but using online world for info.**
- **Making videos and other online activity.**

The Tiger Parent
This is a mother of four, the eldest three are now at university.

I would describe my parenting style as 'tiger mom' when it comes to the internet/digital media – I'm constantly trying to turn them onto ways of using it to empower themselves rather than waste their time. I encourage them to use it as a tool to make their work better, creativity more fun, connections faster – make an arrangement with a friend, then go and meet them in person. We use it for everything at home – homework, referencing anything in a discussion, showing each other Youtube clips, sending each other links – it's an integral part of family life and communication.

They are really into podcasts and always streaming music, using software to compose music – I really encourage creative usage. I'm making them sound very virtuous but there will be stuff that I don't know about – all you can do is talk about it, pornography, violence etc. I ask them to tell me about anything that they've seen that bothered them, but they are far too superior to me – unless I caught them doing it, I have to trust that it's fine!

A big change in my attitude came when I did a teaching course where I had to use an ultranet, online portal, forums, peer learning; it was all tied up with the computer so I wouldn't have understood it unless I'd done that. When they were younger, I would tell them to look at books but now I've accepted that they can work with multiple tabs open, going back and forth – but they are bright kids who can use the internet like that, though they still get distracted. We talk about that, trying not to receive messages when you're focusing, learning how to block things out.

Of course there are still conflicts over time spent online. When they need to get off it to do x, y, or z, they'll always have an argument that 'I'm just making this arrangement, I'm just waiting for them to get back to me' – there's always a reason to have the computer on permanently. My strategy is just to go on at them until they get cross.

We didn't do if for our oldest son – he bought a computer and put it in his room, and that was the living end for him – he then was totally addicted. Now it's all he does – he's like one of those Japanese boys they find in their bedrooms who haven't been out for days – he's been away at university so I have no idea what he does online and he won't tell me. I think boys are particularly prone to this type of social isolation – you're having a social life but online so not actually going out. I can see how it happens, though – I am very addicted myself since getting an iphone. I've also been challenged about having my phone in the bedroom while telling them they can't have computers in their rooms...

Other strategies I've used in the past have been to take the router with me in my handbag when I've gone out. I know families where the internet is turned off at a certain time in the evening. We also have no phones at the dinner table – but [eldest] always has his on him and ends most conversations with looking up something, but then it does mean he's interacting with his brothers so I'm more relaxed about that.

We've also never bought them their own computers – it's amazing how quickly they earn the money for that! We've also never bought an X-box so that's been a major difference between them and friends; but they never seemed that bothered about it and have now pretty much grown out of that phase; I wouldn't have allowed them to buy an X-box even if they had bought it with own money. They did try online gaming with friends but needed a more powerful computer and it defeated them.

We just keep talking about usage – making it more about empowerment. We watch Ted talks together about issues and I show them different artists that I like – to me, it's more about encouraging positive ways of using it. [Third child] got an ipad and starting doing his own animations – we talk about doing more interesting things on computers than just Minecraft. He did have a group of friends with which he entered animations into competitions, doing it all over world, but then it was quite difficult because the relationships were on Skype and phones so I had to monitor that a bit more.

I don't really know if anyone's stricter than me. When the youngest (14) goes for sleepovers, he's a bit overwhelmed with their computer addictions – there was one place where the parents let them stay up all night and watch whatever (he said he took himself off to bed). I think you have to be very onguard if they're younger – and not afraid to ask what the evening will involve, internet usage, films they're going to watch if you're interacting with other families that aren't as strict – you have to be brave and not afraid to ask. I know some parents who have just given up, if a child is particularly wilful or quirky.

Summary

- **No computers in bedrooms, but encouragement for using them to interact with the real world.**
- **Monitoring children's sleepovers to make sure there is some oversight over online involvement.**
- **No gaming consoles.**

The Negotiator Parent

Our subject here is a married father in his fifties with two boys, the eldest of which is twelve.

It is easy to imagine in interviews like this that we have always got everything right and, in practice, I have made very many mistakes. But most of the time – apart from the occasional explosion – we get by.

Both my partner and I start from position of suspicion about most online worlds and the technology behind them, but perhaps for different reasons: me because I am instinctively suspicious of anything that is pushed on our children by the biggest companies, which don't have our needs at heart, and my partner because she would prefer the children to spend more time outside.

I want them reading; she wants them playing. The two together generally mean a meeting of minds, but it is true that my partner tends to be the most insistent that they should not obsess about the online world, or hide behind their phones when they could be taking part in conversation or interacting with the real world.

The children were both fascinated by technology as soon as they could walk, and possibly before. That initial conversation has continued in different ways ever since, partly because it seems to go on at school: about what kinds of computers or consoles at home or phones in their pockets. When they could use the computer, their friends were already doing online games, initially Minecraft.

But it was clear early on that total abstinence was not going to work, if we weren't going to turn our children into social pariahs. Our original plan was that they should get fifteen minutes online gaming every other day, but it was clear pretty quickly that this didn't work. It put such a strain of expectation on those fifteen minutes that it added to the enormous stress that children face anyway when they are trying to master intractable technology.

So it soon became twenty minutes every day and then half an hour every day – which is, generally speaking, where it has remained until the early teens of the eldest. But once you embark on this kind of negotiation, it seems to spread like tentacles into everything.

There are negotiations about the phone once the eldest had one (once he was coming home from school alone). There were negotiations about how to make sure they didn't creep up to the computer during the afternoon or on their way to the bathroom (they objected, quite reasonably, to timers on the modem). There were negotiations about avoiding saying anything about computer restrictions in the hearing of their friends, because the idea of anyone else knowing that their family restricts their computer time as anathema.

This is despite that fact that it is obvious most of their friends also have their computer time restricted, though often in ways that are hard to fathom. It is just that home behaviour needs to match up with at-school bravado.

There were also negotiations along similar lines about what happens if they have to look after themselves for a few hours – and it seemed that some discretion there was the better part of valour. Also about whether there could be special extensions for playing online with friends (there can).

The sum total of all this negotiation is that they must finish homework, chores, music practice, reading and so on before going online. I know they chafe at these restrictions and regard them as an embarrassing weakness in their back story, but I would like to think that it works. It isn't tidy and it doesn't avoid arguments – in fact most of the arguments in the house, including those between my partner and myself, are related in some way or other to the children's time online.

We recently tried to organise a no-screen day once a week and this seems to work, though the children usually start by being resentful. The key, it seems to me, is to make it a special occasion – to have something exciting to eat and to end the evening with a film. If this seems paradoxical, I don't think it is: the children watch almost no television at all, certainly compared to my own generation – and it makes sense to us to be flexible about this. They seem, says my partner, to retain a distant memory of life as it was before they went online, and it was fun – and they fall back on this.

The difficulty with negotiation is that it is never final. I don't know how this arrangement will last as the children get older and our authority wanes – and whether they will develop more self-control and enjoyment of real life before it does. I do know the whole atmosphere will have to shift, slowly I hope, in the next few years. There will also have to be a great deal more negotiation.

Summary

- **Important to stay flexible and to keep on negotiating as things change and the children get older.**
- **The core idea – that they must stay engaged with real life – is never up for negotiation.**
- **No-screen days need to be celebrated with treats or films because they are special times.**

The Low-Tech Parent
Interview with teachers' assistant and mother of two, daughter Rachel (10) and son Tom (8).

I take a very old-fashioned parenting approach, in thinking that they don't need iphones, ipads or any other type of technology.

As parents, both of us want to keep technology out of their lives for as long as possible. We're planning to hold firm on this, at least until secondary school then I'm not sure what we'll do. I don't think it's interesting or important – I want them to be out and about in the garden, or playing imaginary games

– what a childhood should be.

Part of the problem is that they think they need to keep up with other kids – but I've made it clear that I don't care what other parents are doing. The other day they came home from school and wanted to dress up as pirates – the game went on all evening and they looked amazing (I posted a photo on Facebook - I appreciate the irony!)

It can get a bit tiring reiterating this message – we've been doing this for the last four years at least, and the intensity of requests has increased as they've got older, and their friends are doing more online. My son's two best friends are into Minecraft and other computer games – when they come to play, after about half an hour they ask if they can go on the computer because they don't know what else to do. But now they know that it's not an option at our house, they just get on with playing games.

In the last six months, computers have become a really big thing at school with both kids learning how to do assignments on Powerpoint. They were very excited and I was quite impressed with what they were able to do, but it became quite obsessive and we ending up confining screen-time to 30 minutes – and not every day. It would be nice if the school were as enthusiastic about encouraging them to read books!

I work as a teachers' assistant (TA) in a secondary

school and I was quite vocal about how much the children [with special needs] that I was helping needed computers. The arguments for this are that many of them struggle with forming letters – I have accepted this, but still feel that it dilutes learning – it can get a bit chaotic and they are allowed to get out their own phones if the computers aren't free, which is dangerous.

I do get into trouble with the family about sneaking a peak at my phone; the children see the phone as a rival for my attention, although obviously want to go on it themselves. I appreciate the addictive nature of Facebook, and can see that I'm sometimes being hypocritical, having a look at what people have posted. I can also see it might be difficult if most of your other friends have things; that you feel like you're missing out on fun, and that it's also not cool if your mum's stopping you.

We had a conversation about it just a couple of days ago, with Rachel in tears about not having a phone. But I also think it's incredibly sad if getting one is the most exciting thing she has to look forward to.

I've read articles about the detrimental effect that so much screentime is having on society, especially children – I think it's very sinister that they are ever behind a screen. One thing I read recently that made an impression was how people under 30 don't have any empathy, because they're experiencing everything through a false world without having to go through those awkward moments in human interaction.

You do sometimes find, for example in a café, that people are talking to you like a robot – you can see that they are looking at their phones next to the till.

Summary

- **Holding firm with your own beliefs – and don't give in to what other parents are doing.**
- **Encouraging imaginative games – and for other children when they come to play.**
- **Being prepared to review everything at secondary school.**

Grown-up conflicts

One of the more painful aspects of the conversations we have had are about how, in practice, families deal with the online issue is the obvious conflict between partners. It is one of those issues that, like money or discipline, that tend to drive partners apart – and may do even if there is no fundamental disagreement between them.

Years ago, one of the authors of this book got a clue about this from interviewing a money psychologist in the USA about how money can drive a wedge into relationships, and often for the very same reason that online restriction does – because, in both cases, they are given a special significance. Money and gaming are simply means to an end.

If a husband equates money with security and his wife equates money with love, then serious complications will probably follow. The money therapist Olivia Mellan quoted the story of one of her patients, who spent three days before his wedding anniversary looking for the record of the song he had danced to when he met his wife. She was furious that he had spent so little money on her; he felt unappreciated, and so would we.

In most relationships, said Olivia Mellan, one partner is the hoarder and the other the spender. The two sides attack each other, but often turn out to have a secret admiration for the other's qualities: hoarders admire their partners' spontaneity and generosity; spenders admire their partners' self-discipline. Both are afraid to admit this to each other in case it encourages the other. People often play a different role in different relationships: sometimes the hoarder, sometimes the spender.

There are other dualities in our relationships as well, she said. One partner is often a money worrier, and another is a money avoider who keeps piles of unpaid bills under the bed. One partner is a 'money monk' and the other is a 'money lover'. In Britain, we are a nation of money monks. We find money distasteful, disturbing and scarce. It bothers us. The bills are always high, the supply nearly running out.

Worried Chancellors and Prime Ministers preach at us, reinforcing the preaching we inflict on ourselves. "We cannot pay ourselves more than we earn," said Margaret Thatcher over and over again. It is the same with attitudes to children and the online world. One partner becomes the enforcer, the other one becomes the liberaliser, even if they basically agree with each other. They push each other in opposite directions, aware that they also admire the other's stance – but, again, they dare not say so in case it encourages them.

There may be a difference between men and women. The women we met were more likely to be stricter about online involvement, and keener that their children should go outside or play in the old-fashioned way. The men tended to see the importance of chilling out, or perhaps – to be more cynical – to chill out themselves by getting the children online, quiet and out of the way. But these are often tiny differences in emphasis that get exaggerated in practice.

Similar conflicts happen with grandparents. We heard of grandparents who insist on children leaving phones behind at the front door or who find the whole attitude of their own children to their grandchildren's access to the online world incomprehensible.

Again, these differences may actually be very minor, but they cause divisions and stresses and they can be upsetting to all those involved.

A few conclusions

What was fascinating to us is that, although these different people started out with very different attitudes to the online world, and their children's time in it, they have ended in practice not that far apart.

They resist but they also give and take. They keep the conversations going. They think about it and they learn. It is a two-way process.

In short, it may not really be necessary for us to feel alone, as if we were holding back a tide generated by internet corporations, governments and schools alike. All we need do is to talk a little more loudly, and a little less confidentially to each other. We need to band together a little better for courage.

"I do get carried away online and I do enjoy
it, but it is probably right that there are some
restrictions so that I don't get too carried away."
Boy, 12, interviewed for this book

If you have been wondering who is now aspiring to educate our children, then let me introduce you to Bobby Kotick, chief executive of Activision Blizzard and now the tenth best paid CEO in the USA (he earned a package in 2016 worth $33.1 million). He has also been in post since 1991, which makes him the longest serving head of any public tech company in the world.

The company is going through good times these days, with revenue at a record high last year of $6.6 billion, earned partly from their long-running military game Call of Duty. Their new fast-moving action and shooting game Overwatch only launched in May 2016 and, within a year, 30 million gamers had paid $1 billion to play it – including some of our younger relatives, and probably yours too.

If you are largely on Kotick's side, perhaps because you have invested in his company, then this may excite you. It is good to see tech savvy success, after all. If you are more sceptical about the value of gaming, then you might find the 43 billion hours spent playing their games in 2016, by around 450 million people worldwide, as the most gigantic waste of time.

Our own attitudes as parents are probably somewhere between the two, but – as parents – we feel we need to know this. We need to understand the huge economic power wielded by companies like Activision Blizzard to get their 'great hooks' (the phrase is Fortune magazine's) into the minds of our children.

Since the new Overwatch League, a major investment to turn the game into an international sporting event, will stream for six-hour sessions, it implies that Kotick does not share Steve Jobs' determination to protect his children from the online world (though it is fair to say that we don't actually know). What we do know is that he is dating another doyenne of the online corporate universe, Sheryl Sandberg, Facebook's chief operating officer.

The implications of the fact of Activision Blizzard, and the knowledge of the power they want to have over our children, suggests to us that – at the very least – we need to arm ourselves with a plan. This is the one that seems to emerge from all the people we have talked to, and especially from the parents, in the course of researching and writing this book. Just a few conclusions so far:

- Abandoning our children to the online world, even with safeguards against abuse and bullying, can corrode their confidence, their mental health and their imagination.

- Regulating their interaction with technological devices is difficult, and it is best – but not always possible – to start young.

- Standing out for some kind of constraint is particularly tough, and risks alienating your children from their peers – though, in our experience, striking the right balance will not do so.

We need a new social movement of 'digital temperance', says the New York Times. We agree, and this is how they put it:

"Used within reasonable limits, of course, these devices also offer us new graces. But we are not using them within reasonable limits. They are the masters; we are not. They are built to addict us, as the social psychologist Adam Alter's new book Irresistable points out — and to madden us, distract us, arouse us and deceive us. We primp and perform for them as for a lover; we surrender our privacy to their demands; we wait on tenterhooks for every 'like'. The smartphone is in the saddle, and it rides mankind."

So how should we swap places, and put parents – on behalf of their children – back in the saddle. Here is our ten-point plan. It will not suit every family, and certainly not every child, but it will we hope encourage parents who want to lay down rules, but are not sure what, at least that they are not alone.

1. Avoid confrontations through family discussion and negotiation.

There may be exceptions to this in any household, but it makes sense to negotiate the rules with your children – aware that they will need to change every year or so. Most important, it makes sense to try and break through the anger around the issue in many households by explaining why you are concerned.

Many parents get cross at excess and just turn everything off, and encourage the idea that taking computers away is a kind of punishment. It means that addicted children have to face going cold turkey, and it is hardly surprising that – without a sense of love and support – they will be cross.

They may be cross anyway, but they do need to be told as often as possible why some kind of constraint is necessary – but some kind of access too, to make sure they don't binge on it when the constraints are finally taken away.

There can be too little time, especially if it is at

a set time every week, when children will – as the Guardian writer Charles Arthur put it – dissolve sometimes into "agitated clock-watching distraction" as the time approaches and they are stuck in traffic far from home.

Both partners need to keep up a united front, as far as possible, and that implies that they need to do some negotiating too. Otherwise the stricter parent will feel left out and the more permissive parent will find their boundaries being particularly tested by the children. It is even more difficult for a single parent, who may find themselves the sole focus of emotional outbursts and rage. But then, so it is with any kind of restraint.

All you can do is to remind your children that you love them and want them to be happy, and you know that too much on-screen life will undermine that. They might not agree, but they will recognise and feel ashamed of outbursts in the past and they know that too much time online can corrode their mood, and lead them to be that much more obsessive later.

If they have given up activities they love just to be on a screen, or they are too tired because they have sneaked off to play at night and in the early hours of the morning, they need to be reminded.

Probably this kind of negotiation, which is at least human and dignified, is better than the apps

(DinnerTime or ScreenTime) which can block your children from using a mobile phone at the click of a button.

2. Set times when the computer goes on or the router goes off.

At long last, some of the arms of government are beginning to take an interest in this issue. The American Academy of Paediatrics says there should be no screen time at all for children under the age of 18 months, followed by a maximum of one hour a day up to the age of five. In the UK, the National Institute for Health and Care Excellence (Nice) suggests that children should have TV-free days, or alternatively that they should have two-hour limits on the time spent in front of screens. Other people suggest 90 minutes.

The best stories seem to suggest half an hour to an hour, after homework and music practice, maybe after some form of exercise. It may be that you will negotiate some kind of timing device on the router so that it goes off at a certain time, but the sheer inflexibility – and the lack of trust – inherent in that kind of measure does make it more difficult to sustain. Our advice is that you leave the timer in reserve for when you need it.

Too much control may also undermine their self-control, so there is going to be a continual negotiation over how to make sure these timetables are kept to. With phones, once they reach secondary school age they arguably need one, but perhaps only in the week to start with, or until they can show some restraint in its use.

It may be that a better way is to give them a weekly number of hours, perhaps four or five, and give them the task of allocating it as they want. Whether you choose that or not, it may also make sense to let them play longer some evenings when they are playing online with friends. There are still drawbacks to this, but at least it is a social activity involving communication, give and take.

It makes sense for everyone to know the time limit at the start of each session and to give them a five-minute warning – and to be flexible and reasonable even then. Children get furious when you cut them off suddenly – and you can see why – but it may be that you have to once or twice, just to show you can.

3. Have screen-free days.

You hear sad stories in newspapers from families who find themselves marooned, even if it is only in a holiday cottage with a broken router, when – after the panic has subsided – the whole family finds joy in some of the ordinary, creative or joint activities that they used to love before the advent of screens. Why is it sad? Because invariably they go back home to their previous one-dimensional existence.

Going cold turkey is a risky business, fraught with rage, guilt and self-disgust. And it turns your children into recovering addicts even when they were no such thing. But you can have a creative burst of turkey every week by instituting a screen-free day once a week, or perhaps – if that is too difficult – once a fortnight.

The only issue is what you help your children do instead. There are excellent books for younger children, involving a great deal of sellotape (see How to Unplug Your Child by Liat Hughes Joshi). For older children, it seems to us that the best prescription is to create a sense of occasion – to go somewhere, have a trip, make a favourite meal, have friends round (if the whole concept of a screen-free day is not too embarrassing), have a party or watch a film in front of the fire. Should screen-free extend to mobiles and television? Not necessarily – we are not purists and TV is a surprisingly social medium. It has to be fun and memorable and, eventually, they will look forward to it.

Our children greet the prospect of a screen-free day with some gloom, it is true. But it is surprising how quickly they break out of it and remember –

deep down perhaps – that there was a time when they loved the real world.

4. Have a computer set up in the kitchen, not in bedrooms.

Safety online is beyond the scope of this book, important as it is. But for this as well, it makes sense to make sure computer equipment is visible. This is much more difficult with phones, which is why it is important to have a clear turn-off moment every evening.

Even if portable computers or tablets are sometimes in bedrooms, it is important that they are not owned individually. They should live in a busy room, where people pass to and fro and they should be available for homework there.

Other people may disagree about where homework should be done, but there are disadvantages about doing it in bedrooms. It can make bedrooms places of study rather than rest. It can make sleep difficult. If it means that computer leisure time gets hidden away, that is also not very healthy. We need to bring it out of the shadows.

5. Model the kind of online behaviour you want to see in your children.

This may mean a simple proposition: if you want

your children to get a life, you need to get a life yourself. If you think a phone message, a tweet, a text or an instagram is more important than family meals, conversations with kids or being in the moment, then that is the lesson your children will draw from it.

We are aware that this is not an easy strategy and it is pretty simple to find yourself being overly-sanctimonious about it, but the truth is that is important. The truth also is that most parents get caught in this way and we are both aware that we have lessons we still need to learn before we have cracked this one without hypocrisy.

It may be that we have to look more unflinchingly at our own lives here to see why the online world has such a grip on our children's lives. It is all very well criticising children who sense that the world of online games or social media is shinier, glitzier, more exciting and more fulfilling, when – deep down – we also fear that this is the case too.

Part of the problem here is that mobile phones have become a symbol of access to the adult world, and a great deal of what our children see all around them will simply confirm that all truth, all thrills and all life emanates through the small screen. This is an adolescent fantasy which, in some ways, we remain enslaved to. Our own families and our lives at home can seem to pale into dullness in comparison.

The answer, if there is one, is to see how we all suffer to a greater or lesser extent from this delusion and to find ways of acting differently.

6. Regulate the kinds of games your children play.

We intrude into our children's watching habits at our peril, but we have to go there sometimes just because we are parents. We need to know the level of violence that prevail in the worlds they live in, and we need to know the kind of attitudes and language used by favourite online programmes – even if it would bore us to tears to watch them.

Again, it would be glib to say this is easy. Nor do we necessarily need to censor them, depending on their age and what they are watching. But it may be necessary, if they are particularly young, to note that the depth of cynicism – or the language – in their Youtube forays – need some balance, or at least comment.

There are too many Youtube channels that display more worldweariness and nihilism than they would if they realised most of their viewers were eleven years old. You may not mind four-letter words – until you realise your eight-year-old is likely to repeat them in class.

As for the games themselves, it makes sense to set out some yardsticks whereby it is reasonably obvious to your children what games they will be allowed and what they will not. Perhaps it involves no first-person shooting games. Perhaps it will involve no first-person shooters with guns. Perhaps it will be something about the speed of the games. There is all the difference in the world between Minecraft and Call of Duty, after all. One can be constructive, the other is unremittingly destructive.

The futurist John Naisbitt has written widely about what he dubbed the 'Military-Nintendo Complex', which he used to describe the close affinity and links between military trainers and games designers. It maybe that we could turn a blind eye to the bludgeoning to death of some furry creatures in Lord of the Rings Online. We would find it difficult, though, to accept some of the face-to-face killing of human beings – even with the blood 'turned off' – in Call of Duty or Grand Theft Auto.

It may not matter where precisely you draw the line. It will anyway be made less precise as children push at the boundaries, which is only to be expected. Nor does it matter if the line meanders a little when children visit friends. But we do think a line will need to be drawn, just as most people would draw a line about what films they would allow their children to watch. It is the same with games – and maybe even more so. Movies only involve what our children see;

games also involve what they are encouraged to do.

7. Put all the family's mobile phones away before 8pm.

We are only too aware that this rule is not enough to prevent youngsters being glued to their phones most of the day. It may be that you would go further and collect up the phones when people come in the front door, or before they sit down for a meal. But as a bare minimum, it seems to us that all the mobile phones in the house should be put together in the kitchen for charging a little time before bed.

It is important that this applies to everyone's phone. This may occasionally be inconvenient, and particularly so if you work shifts, but at least children must know that the rules on phones apply to everybody.

8. Reward reading time.

This may be the most controversial of all the suggestions here. There is a view among some parents that you should not make going online the subject of discipline or sticks and carrots. We can see what they mean but, even so, it seems to us that it makes sense to let reading – of books, that is – be a trigger that can allow online time to happen.

It is true that you don't want reading to seem like

any kind of punishment or chore, but this may be the best way to make sure it happens at all. It makes us weep when children who were keen readers set it all aside to play online games. There has to be an antidote. It seems to us sensible not to allow your children online until they have read.

It makes sense also to let then choose what to read – to insist that they enjoy it too. There is nothing worse than clock-watching while you are reading. But we fully understand why you may not follow us down this particular path.

9. Forgive yourself and chill out.

This is no exact science. Every child and every family will be different and it is the direction of travel that counts, not individual discrepancies and failures of the new regime. When you set yourselves up against the will of the multi-billionaire Lords of the Internet, you are not going to win all the time, and it makes no sense to beat yourself up when you fail or it doesn't work.

The important thing is to learn when things go wrong, and to adapt accordingly. It is particularly hit or miss when you are constructing rules for and with rather older children.

The chances are that your children are just online, even quite a lot, primarily because it is fun and – or so it seems – that it is a strategy for tackling boredom. This may be nonsense, but it does not make them ill or deviant or addicts. They are probably perfectly charming and able to navigate in the real world as well as anyone else their age. So don't punish yourself when it fails to work – and especially don't reflect their obsessions with gaming or social media with an obsession with them not going there from their parents.

10. Celebrate more.

We have wondered why it is so often in the cities of the Far East where young people become so addicted to their online lives that they die at their screens. China's National People's Congress has estimated that 10 per cent of China's Internet users under eighteen years old are addicted, which they define as being online more than six hours a day. Recently, there was one case of a father sending his addicted son to a Chinese screen addiction camp, where he was beaten to death by one of the guards. Why is the situation so extreme in Eastern cities?

It is at least possible that fake environments, high rise living and alienation from the natural world – living in a shiny, ersatz world – can increase the temptation to lose yourself in a fake online world instead. It is hard to know.

What we can know is that there may be a duty on us parents to show our children how to live better, despite the time and economic pressures that hem us in. That may not always be possible. We can't organise treats and celebrations all the time. But we need to do so just a little more, to celebrate, sing, party and play in as authentic a way as possible. To demonstrate that the real world may be inconvenient, it may often be dull, but it can also be magnificent.

It goes without saying that there are also very important things that any parent should do to keep children safe online. As discussed before, that is not the subject of this book, but we include some online resources for advice on this at the end of the book, in the Resources section.

Postscript

Go to the cinema these days, and the first twenty minutes of the programme will usually include two or three expensively made advertisements attempting to convince us that there is a world of hyper-reality available only through mobile telephony.

But a visit to the Hay Festival in the sweltering early summer of 2017 convinced us that something else may be happening with technology. There we were in the green room with the writers and television personalities, scientists and historians – some of the most successful and influential people in the nation, and something was very clear. Almost none of them were using phones or ipads and tablets.

In fact, there was little or no sign of any electronic gadgets at all. It struck us that this may be the way the trend is moving: a class divide is opening up, between those who wed themselves to their phones and those who consider themselves to be beyond that kind of thing.

This does not strike us as a healthy trend, involving class in what is already a delicate balance, but it is a potentially transformative shift. We have seen the future, and it looks as though it is tiring of gadgets.

Find out more

Adam Alter (2017), Irresistible: Why We Can't Stop Checking, Scrolling, Clicking and Watching, Vintage.

Teresa Belton (2014), Happier People, Healthier Planet, Silverwood.

Mine Conkbaier (2017), Early Childhood and Neuroscience:
Theory, Research and Implications for Practice, Bloomsbury.

Digital Detox, www.digitaldetox.org

Victoria Dunkley (2015), 'Screentime is making kids moody, crazy and lazy', Psychology Today, 18 Aug.

Liat Hughes-Joshi (2015), How to Unplug your Child, Vie.
See also: www.liathughesjoshi.co.uk

International Gaming Research Unit www.ntu.ac.uk/research/groups-and-centres/the-international-gaming-research-unit

Noel Janis-Norton (2016), Calmer, Easier Happier Screentime, Yellow Kite. See also www.calmerparenting.com

Stuart Shankar (2011), Self-Reg: How to help your child and you break the stress cycle and successfully engage with life, Hachette.

Aric Sigman (2011), The Spoilt Generation: Standing up to our demanding children, Hachette.

Catherine Steiner-Adair (2013), The Big Disconnect: Protecting Childhood and Family Relationships in the Digital Age, HarperCollins.

Unplugged Weekend, www.unpluggedweekend.com

Jonathan Wells (2016), 'Nine ways to start and stick to a digital detox', Daily Telegraph, 1 June.

Zoe Williams (2014), 'Game on or off?' The Guardian, 31 Jan.

Online safety

www.childnet.com/sns
www.internetmatters.org
www.nspcc.org.uk/onlinesafety
www.parentzone.org.uk
www.thinkyouknow.co.uk/parents
www.askaboutgames.com

Other HOW TO books from the Real Press

How to become a freelance writer

This is a manual about freelance writing with a difference. It won't tell you how to write or what to write. It assumes you know these things already. It doesn't set out to equip you for a brief period of freelancing.

It will, on the other hand, tell you how to go about living a writer's life in a practical way – how to plan ahead, how to shape your career, how to find clients and how to deal with the money. It will tell you how to make a life out of writing without falling into the many little traps that are set for us once we embark on the idea.

If you are thinking of changing your life, you may be tempted to buy many other books about how to write, or taking the first technical steps into becoming a freelancer – but this book will set you on the path to live that life.

Why not build your own strategy

www.ingramcontent.com/pod-product-compliance
Lightning Source LLC
Chambersburg PA
CBHW021205020426
42331CB00003B/216